let's play with
Paper

Ivan Bulloch & Diane James

World Book

in association with

TWOCAN

Art Director Ivan Bulloch
Editor Diane James
Illustrator Emily Hare
Photographer Daniel Pangbourne
Models Imaarl, Alicia, Kaz, Maryam, Cory, Jasmin, Abigail,
Kerri, Courtney, Eleanor, Shaniqua

Special thanks to Sharon Nowakowski, World Book Publishing

First published in the United States and Canada by
World Book, Inc.
525 W. Monroe
Chicago, IL 60661
in association with Two-Can Publishing Ltd.

**For information on other World Book products,
call 1-800-255-1750, x 2238,
or visit our Web site at http://www.worldbook.com**

Library of Congress Cataloging-in-Publication Data
Bulloch, Ivan.
    Let's play with paper/Ivan Bulloch & Diane James: [illustrator, Emily
Hare; photographer, Daniel Pangbourne].
       p.   cm.
    Summary: Provides step-by-step instructions and illustrations for a
variety of craft projects with paper.
    ISBN 0-7166-5606-X (hc). — ISBN 0-7166-5607-8 (sc)
    1. Paper work—Juvenile literature. [1. Paper work. 2. Handicraft.]
I. James, Diane. II. Hare, Emily, ill. III. Pangbourne, Daniel, ill. IV. Title.
TT870.B84 1998
745.54—dc21   97-26502

Printed in Spain
1 2 3 4 5 6 7 8 9 10 01 00 99 98 97

Contents

snip and stick

Did you know you can make a picture without paints or pencils? You just need paper, scissors, and glue! Plan a picture in your head first. Will your picture have people, animals, flowers, or buildings? Or will it be a pattern?

1 Collect lots of different kinds of paper—newspaper, tissue, colored paper, and colorful pages from old magazines—get permission.

2 Use a large sheet of paper for the background. When you have decided what your picture is going to be, start cutting or tearing your paper shapes. Always use safety scissors, like the ones in the picture.

Cut it out ...

4 When you are happy with how your paper picture looks, glue the shapes in place. Firmly press down on all the shapes to stop the edges from curling up. You can use a rolling pin to help!

3 Place your paper shapes on the background paper to make your picture. Don't worry about changing your mind and rearranging the shapes. Sometimes second or third ideas are best!

...and stick it down!

secret scrapbook

Where do you keep all your favorite pictures and photos? If the answer is, "in an untidy pile," or "hidden in a cardboard box," it's time you made yourself a scrapbook! You can put your pictures in the book and enjoy them whenever you feel like it.

Show me yours!

1 Decide how many pages you want in your scrapbook. Cut the pages out of colored paper, making sure they are all the same size.

2 Use a hole punch to make two holes on the side of each page. Make sure the holes are in the same place on every page. You can punch holes in two or three sheets at the same time.

OK! Let's share secrets.

3 Decorate the cover by gluing on shapes cut from colored paper. Or you can use pictures cut from a magazine, but don't forget to ask first!

4 Get two pieces of thin ribbon or cord. Stack your pages on top of each other with the cover on top. Thread the ribbons through the holes and tie a bow. Now, start gluing your pictures onto the pages!

pretty pots

Here is an easy way to make an extra-special gift! First you'll need a plant in a pot. Make sure the outside of the pot is clean and dry. Follow the instructions and make a colorful wrapper for the pot.

1 Measure the length around the top of your pot using a long piece of string. Cut a strip of paper about half as long again. The paper should be as deep as the pot.

2 Decorate the paper by gluing on simple shapes cut from different colored paper.

I made this just for you!

3 Start at one end of the strip and fold the paper backward and forward until you reach the other end. Make the folds exactly the same size each time.

glue

4 Gently wrap the folded paper around the flower pot and glue the edges together. Your present is ready!

9

party decorations

All you have to do is make a few simple folds, a couple of snips with your scissors, and "presto," you'll have some great decorations to cheer up the party!

Don't pull too hard!

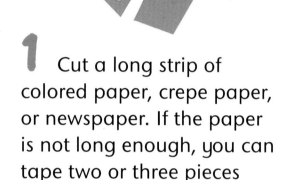

1 Cut a long strip of colored paper, crepe paper, or newspaper. If the paper is not long enough, you can tape two or three pieces together.

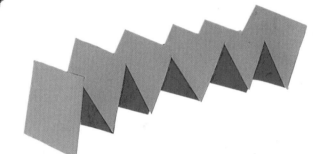

2 Start at one end of the strip, and fold the paper backward and forward until you reach the other end. The fold should be big enough for you to draw half of a shape on it—for example, half of a rabbit or half of a butterfly shape.

3 Keep your paper folded and draw half of a shape on the top page. The center of your shape should be on the folded edge. Make sure that one part of your shape touches the edge that is opposite the fold.

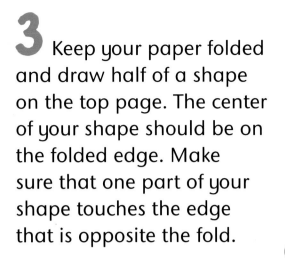

Just a bit higher!

4 Ask a grown-up to help cut along your drawn lines—through all the layers—taking care not to cut too much of the folded edge. Unfold your shape and hang your long decoration!

paper beads

You don't need to spend all your pocket money on real jewelry. It's easy to make necklaces from bits of colored paper! When you're not wearing your beads, hang them up to decorate your room.

1 Glue two different colored sheets of paper together. Press them together firmly.

2 When the glue is dry, tear triangles from it. Don't worry about the rough edges. Make as many triangles as you can from your sheet.

It's just like the real thing!

3 Starting with the wide end, wind a triangle around a thick pencil or marker. When you get to the end, glue the tip of the triangle down. Slip the bead off the pencil. Make lots more beads in the same way.

4 Thread your beads onto thick cord or ribbon. Ask an adult to tie your necklace loosely around your neck.

13

paper pulp

It's hard to believe, but you really can make a big bowl using newspaper, water, and some PVA glue. There are also lots of other things you can make when you know how to mix up this gooey paper pulp.

Perfect...

...for pencils!

1 Tear four or five large sheets of newspaper into small pieces. Put them in a bucket and pour in enough water to cover them.

2 Leave the newspaper to soak overnight. Squish the pieces together with your hands and pour out the leftover water. Add three or four big squirts of PVA glue and mix well with a wooden spoon.

3 Use a large bowl as a mold (use a jar or glass if you want to make a pencil holder). Cover it with plastic wrap. Take small handfuls of pulp and press them onto the mold.

4 When the mold is covered, let the pulp dry. This can take three or four days. Then, lift the paper bowl off the mold. You can paint your bowl in your favorite colors.

Looking good!

15

hide and seek!

Would you like to be a black-and-white panda or a spotted monster? You can be anything you like when you make your own fun mask!

Bet you can't guess who I am!

1 Draw and then cut a mask shape, slightly wider than your face, from poster board. Leave room for your nose to poke out at the bottom!

2 Ask a grown-up to measure how far apart your eyes are, and then to help cut holes in your mask so you can see. Now it's time to decorate your mask.

3 Cut out shapes from colored paper and glue them onto your mask.

Here comes the spotted monster!

4 Ask a grown-up to make a small hole on each side of your mask. Poke a piece of string or ribbon through each hole and make a knot. Find a friend to help tie the mask around your head.

17

fruity cakes!

Paper cakes are a lot easier to make than the real thing. The only problem is you can't eat them! Think of all your favorite toppings—cream, chocolate, cherries—and add them to your cakes. Now give your dolls and teddies a special treat!

1 Gather some cake-shaped boxes—round ones, squares, rectangles, even triangles.

2 Trace around one of the boxes on a sheet of colored paper. Cut out the shape and glue it onto the top of the box.

Not for eating—just for fun!

3 Cut a long strip of colored paper that is the same height as your box. Glue shapes onto one side of the strip or make small folds in it backward and forward. Tape the strip around the box.

4 Now, decorate the top of your cake! Cut shapes of your favorite toppings and glue them onto the cake.

19

clown hats

Why don't you turn yourself into a clown with a funny paper hat and curly paper hair? Add some colorful face paints and put on a funny act for your friends.

Sad clown!

1 Draw a large circle, about 18 inches (45 cm) across, on colored paper. Cut it out and fold it in half. Now cut along the folded line. Decorate one piece by gluing paper shapes onto one side of it. Save the other piece to make another hat later!

20

2 Gently curve your half circle into a cone shape. Tape the edges together. Ask a grown-up to make a hole on each side of your hat. Thread a piece of ribbon through each hole. Tie knots to stop them from sliding through.

3 Tape shredded paper or thick wool inside the hat. Leave space at the front so you can see!

Happy clown!

wrap it up!

Any present will look extra special if it's wrapped in paper that you designed yourself. Put the present in a cardboard box, as this will make it easier to wrap, and no one will guess what's inside!

1 Find a large sheet of plain wrapping paper or colored paper. It should be big enough to wrap around your box.

2 Decide on a pattern and cut some shapes from other colored paper.

Which one would you like?

3 Cut more paper shapes using different colors. Glue all the shapes onto one side of the large sheet of paper.

4 Put your boxed present in the middle of the plain side of the large sheet. Wrap the long sides over the box and tape them down. Tuck both ends in neatly and tape them down. Add ribbons or bows.

23

tips and tricks

Here are some of our favorite tips to help you with your paper crafts.

1 Keep a collection of papers in a big envelope. Even scraps may be useful.

2 To make good, sharp folds, run your fingers up and down each fold carefully.

3 If something goes wrong, don't throw the paper away. Smooth it out and use it again!

4 Use scissors to cut a smooth edge to your paper shapes. If you want a rough edge, tear the paper carefully.

5 When you are gluing shapes onto a piece of paper, press them down firmly for several seconds; count to 10 slowly.

6 If you need extra-strong paper, glue two layers of paper together to make a thicker sheet.